Bite Size

GEOGRAPHY

Bite Size

GEOGRAPHY

150

Facts You Won't Believe!

HUGH WESTRUP

pictures by Jackie Urbanovic

ISBN 0-590-12197-9

12 11 10 9 8 7 6 5 4 3   8 9/9 0 1 2 3/0

Printed in the U.S.A.   01

First Scholastic printing, January 1998

TABLE OF CONTENTS

Introduction	1
North America	3
Australia	15
Asia	21
South America	25
Europe	29
Antarctica	37
Africa	41
The Oceans	47
Did You Know?	51
About the Author	57

Many years ago, when the first explorers set off to see the world, the earth was a very mysterious place. Some explorers expected to encounter dragons swimming in the ocean. Others feared they might reach the edge of the world and fall off.

Today, the world is not as mysterious, but seeing it's as exciting as ever. For this book, I have collected some fascinating facts about the world's landmarks. When you turn the page, imagine yourself a modern-day explorer embarking on your own world adventure. Enjoy the trip!

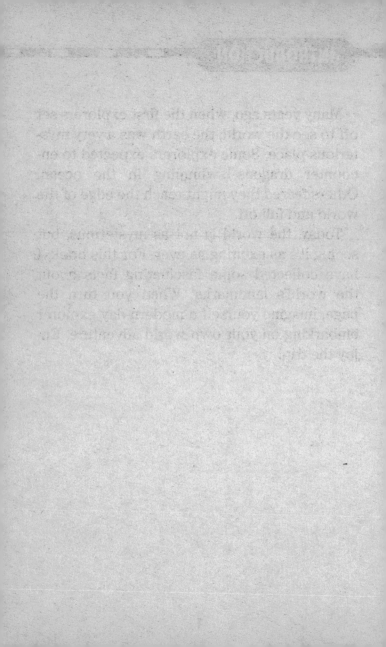

- Four Corners is a spot in the United States where four states meet. You could stand at Four Corners and throw rocks into Arizona, Colorado, New Mexico, and Utah.

- The tiny D River in Oregon is only about as long as a Burger King parking lot.

- Disneyland is located in Orange County, California. Disney World is located in Orange County, Florida.

- A group of hills in northern Canada are chronic smokers. Rock and soil in the cliffs contain substances that react with one another chemically and have given off heat and clouds of white smoke for hundreds of years.

- Fierce bull sharks live in Lake Nicaragua, the largest lake in Central America. Bull sharks grow as long as 9 feet (2.7 meters) and attack almost any living thing, including dogs and people who wade or swim in the lake.

- The longest street in the world is Yonge Street in Canada. It begins in Toronto, the capital of Ontario, and ends 1,178 miles (1,896 kilometers) to the northwest in the town of Rainy River.

- Big gullies in the mountains of central Mexico look like bowling alleys for giants. Strewn across the gulleys are hundreds of huge round boulders made of volcanic rock.

- A desert with sand dunes over 100 feet (30 meters) high exists along the flatlands of the Kobuk River in northwestern Alaska.

- Most U.S. interstate highways that run east and west have even numbers. Most U.S. interstate highways that run north and south have odd numbers.

- Chicago, Illinois, is not one of the windiest cities in the United States. It was nicknamed the Windy City because Chicagoans thought the local politicians were full of "hot air."

- The largest stone pyramid in the world is in Mexico, not Egypt. Called the Quetzalcoatl pyramid, it is located north of Mexico City and was built 1,000 years ago by the Toltec people.

- Half the world's lakes are located in Canada.

- The Reversing Falls on the St. John River in New Brunswick regularly flow backward. The falls are located near to where the river empties into the Bay of Fundy. When the tide rises in the bay, water is forced back up the river and the falls reverse direction.

- About half the states in the United States got their names from Native Indian words. Here is what some of those names mean:

  Oklahoma: "red people"
  Texas: "friends"
  Missouri: "town of large canoes"
  Arizona: "little spring"
  Illinois: "tribe of superior men"
  Kentucky: "land of tomorrow"
  Mississippi: "father of the waters"
  Iowa: "the beautiful land"
  Massachusetts: "great mountain place"
  Alabama: "vegetation gatherers"

- The Moose Dropping Festival happens every year in Talkeetna, Alaska, a small town at the foot of North America's highest mountain, Mt. McKinley. Townspeople wear jewelry made from moose dung for the festival, and have moose-dung throwing contests.

- If you fly due south from the City Airport in Detroit, Michigan, the first foreign country you pass over is Canada.

- Idaho harvests more potatoes than any other state. A field of potatoes in Idaho was struck once by bolts of lightning during a storm. The potatoes, which the lightning cooked to a turn, were dug up and served to people as baked spuds.

- Indiana is said to have got its nickname, the Hoosier State, from an old pioneer greeting, "Who'shyer?" which means "How are you?"

- "The worst jungle in the world" is the Darien Gap in southern Panama. Extremely hot and swampy, the Darien Gap is crawling with large mosquitoes and deadly snakes.

- The biggest garbage dump on Earth is in New York City. It processes 4.368 million tons of garbage each year.

- Niagara Falls is continually wearing away the rocks at its edge. In about 25,000 years' time, Niagara Falls will have worn its way upstream all the way to Lake Erie and disappeared.

- Mexico's Yucatán peninsula got its name when a Spanish explorer asked a Native Indian what the name of the land was. The Indian replied, "I don't understand you," in his native language. The explorer mistook the Indian's reply for the name of the land.

- New Hampshire has a seacoast that is only 10 miles (16 kilometers) long.

• Edward and Emelda Gosselin have lived for 35 years in a house that sits right on the Vermont-Quebec border. They watch TV in the United States, but eat and sleep in Canada!

- The state of Nevada is located east of California, but the city of Reno, Nevada, is located farther west than Los Angeles, California.

- North America has many cities and towns with unusual names. Have you ever been to:
  Truth or Consequences (New Mexico)
  Moose Jaw (Saskatchewan)
  Goodnight (Texas)
  Waterproof (Louisiana)
  Bowlegs (Oklahoma)
  Accident (Maryland)
  Cuckoo (Virginia)
  Tomato (Arkansas)
  Chunky (Mississippi)
  Headquarters (Idaho)

- The windiest city in the United States is Cheyenne, Wyoming. The average wind speed there is 12.9 miles (20.8 kilometers) per hour.

- Death Valley, California, is the hottest and driest place in the United States. It also lies lower than any other spot in the country — 282 feet (86 meters) below sea level.

- A watermelon sitting on a kitchen table in a house in Bentonville, Arkansas, blew up during a thunderstorm in 1987. A clap of thunder caused the melon to vibrate so fast that it exploded.

- The oldest rocks in the United States are 3.6 billion years old. They lie scattered on the ground in southwest Minnesota.

- The state of Louisiana was created almost entirely by the Mississippi River. It is made of bits of soil from other states farther north.

- The soil in Vidalia, Georgia, produces onions so sweet you can eat them like apples.

- More than half of Americans live within an hour's drive of the seashore.

- In 1820, 72 percent of Americans worked on farms. Today, only 2 percent work on farms.

- Extreme summer conditions, such as heat and humidity, make Houston, Texas, and Phoenix, Arizona, the most uncomfortable places to live in the United States, according to the U.S. government.

- The highest U.S. state is Colorado; the lowest is Florida. The highest ground in Florida is only 345 feet (105 meters) above sea level.

- Nineteen out of twenty Australians live south of the line on the map. (see drawing)

- Willy-willies are what Australians call hurricanes.

- No one knows why, but Lake Hillier on Middle Island, Australia, is bright pink in color.

- The Breadknife is a jagged blade of rock that rises 300 feet (91 meters) out of the Warrumbungles, a group of mountains in southeastern Australia. Climbing the Breadknife is so dangerous that it is against the law.

- The world's largest rock is Uluru, a huge dome of red sandstone that rises out of the middle of the Great Australian Desert. At sunset, Uluru seems to burn like a humongous hot coal.

- Australia has only two major rivers, the Murray and the Darling. Both are in the southeastern part of the country.

- A mild electric current 3,750 miles (6,035 kilometers) long runs underground through Australia. One scientist thinks the electric current marks the boundaries where ancient pieces of Earth's crust came together and fused into a single landmass that became Australia.

- Dinosaurs ruled Earth during the Jurassic period. A type of tree that was common during the Jurassic period still lives in Australia. Do you think the tree has Jurassic bark?

- The Bungle Bungles are thousands of tiger-striped rock formations shaped like beehives in northwestern Australia. Some of the Bungle Bungles are as small as houses; others are almost as big as mountains.

- Most of Australia's natural lakes are what geographers call playas. They don't have water for several months or years at a time. They fill with water only after a heavy rain.

- Much of Australia is desert. The early European settlers of Australia were so discouraged by the barren land that they gave landmarks names like Mount Hopeless and Lake Disappointment.

- A cockroach race is held by people in the city of Darwin every January 26, Australia's national holiday. The roaches are timed as they scuttle along the coastline of a big map of Australia.

- The "dingo fence" in Australia is the longest fence in the world. The fence is 3,437 miles (5,531 kilometers) long and helps keep wild dogs called dingoes from getting into the southern part of Australia and killing the many sheep that live there.

- Billabongs are what Australians call watering holes.

- Pigtailed macaque monkeys are employed to pick coconuts on plantations in Thailand. The monkeys have been taught to select only ripe coconuts and to swim after coconuts floating in ponds and streams.

- The busiest McDonald's restaurant in the world is in Beijing, the capital of China.

- Though Malaysia now produces more rubber than any other country in the world, rubber is not a native plant in Malaysia. The country's rubber crop began as 11 trees imported from England in 1877.

- The Chocolate Hills on Bohol, an island in the Philippines, look good enough to eat. The hills, which resemble hundreds of giant haystacks, are brilliant green during the rainy season, but turn chocolate brown from February to May.

- Komodo dragons are huge lizards that inhabit several islands in Indonesia. They eat goats, people, and even other Komodo dragons.

- Lake Baikal in the Russian district of Siberia is thought to be the oldest and deepest lake in the world. It is 25 million years old and 5,371 feet (1,637 meters) deep.

- The wettest place on Earth is Mawsynram, a city in India that gets an average of 467.5 inches (1,187.5 centimeters) of rainfall per year.

- The deadliest earthquake in history happened in China in 1556. It killed 830,000 people.

- The first known city on Earth was Jericho, which today is part of Israel. When it was built 10,000 years ago, Jericho's population was about 3,000.

- More than one-quarter of the world's forests are in Siberia.

- The earliest known map is a clay tablet that is about 4,300 years old. It shows land features and a river in Mesopotamia, an ancient country that is now present-day Iraq.

- Japan is a chain of 3,900 volcanic islands. Sixty volcanoes in Japan are still active.

- Jaisalmer is a medieval fortress-city that sits on the edge of Thar Desert in northern India. The dwellings in the city are made of sandstone, and each evening the setting sun bathes the city in a beautiful golden glow.

- The world's largest cave is the Sarawak Chamber on the island of Borneo. Its ceiling is hundreds of feet high, and it has boulders as big as houses in it.

- The oldest country in the world, Iran, has existed since 529 B.C. It was called Persia until 1934.

- A beauty pageant for burros is held every spring by the townspeople of San Antero in Colombia. The burros parade around in women's dresses and bonnets, and, for the climax of the pageant, wear brightly colored swimsuits.

- Ecuador is so named because it's situated on the equator. *Ecuador* is the Spanish word for the equator.

- The Amazon River contributes one-fifth of all the water that the rivers of the world pour into the oceans.

- The driest desert in the world is the Atacama in northern Chile. Rain has never been recorded in some places there.

- The world's highest large lake is Lake Titicaca in the Andes Mountains of Bolivia and Peru. The local Aymara people build large rafts on the lake and live in houses on the rafts.

- The world's highest waterfall, Angel Falls in Venezuela, is 3,212 feet (979 meters) high. It was named after Jimmy Angel, an American World War II pilot and explorer who spotted the falls from an airplane in 1935.

- High atop a mountainous crag in Peru are the spectacular remains of the ancient city of Machu Picchu. The lords of the great Incan empire are believed to have worshipped their gods at Machu Picchu.

- The southernmost city in the world is Punta Arenas, Chile.

- Pink dolphins live in the Amazon River. The brightly colored mammals look like big wads of swimming bubble gum.

- The biggest spiders in the world live in the countries of Surinam, Guiana, and French Guiana. Called goliath bird-eating spiders because they actually eat birds, they can grow almost 1 foot (30 centimeters) long.

- Brasília, the capital of Brazil, was built 40 years ago in the country's wilderness. From an airplane you can see that Brasília was designed in the shape of a bow and arrow.

- Tepius are 100 flat-topped mountains that rise out of the jungle in southeast Venezuela. In *The Lost World*, a science fiction story written 100 years ago by Sir Arthur Conan Doyle, explorers climb to the top of a tepius and find dinosaurs living there.

- The world's smallest breed of horse, the Falabela, was bred in Argentina. One adult female Falabela stood only 15 inches (38 centimeters) tall and weighed just over 26 pounds (12 kilograms).

- The Penitentes are thousands of sparkling snow spikes, some as high as 20 feet (6 meters), that exist along the Agua Negra Pass between Chile and Argentina in the Andes Mountains.

- If you climb the Harz Mountains in Germany, you might see the Spectre of the Brocken, a giant shadow of yourself cast by the sun onto the sky.

- San Marino is Europe's oldest existing country. It is located in the Apennine Mountains in central Italy and has more teachers for every student than any other country in the world.

- The land in Norway, Sweden, and Finland that lies above the Arctic Circle is called Lapland. The inhabitants of Lapland, the Lapps, are short people who fish, cut timber, and raise reindeer for a living.

- Many sailors have been sucked to their deaths by the huge whirlpools and thrashing waves of the Maelstrom, a savage strait of water in the Lofoten Islands of Norway.

- The Ritten Earth Pillars are bunches of skinny rock spires that rise high above the treetops in the mountains of northern Italy. Many of the jagged spires, which were created by erosion, have a big boulder perched on them. Local people called the pillars "earth mushrooms."

- The Eiffel Tower in Paris is 2.4 inches (6 centimeters) taller on a hot summer day than it is on a cold winter night.

- The French eat more snails than any other people in the world.

- The smallest country in the world, Vatican City, is located in the city of Rome, Italy. Disney World in Florida is 300 times bigger than Vatican City.

- Huff Puff. The longest stairway in the world is in Switzerland. It has 11,674 steps. It follows a railroad track that climbs the side of one of the Alps Mountains.

- Canary birds were named after Spain's Canary Islands, where the little yellow birds were first found. The islands themselves were named thousands of years ago after large, fierce dogs that also live on the islands. The Latin word for dog is *canis*.

- Legoland, a family theme park in Billund, Denmark, was built from 44.5 million Lego bricks. Lego was invented by a Danish carpenter in 1932.

- Wales has many towns with extremely long names. Some of them are Rhosllanerchrugog, Penrhyndeudraeth, Cerrigydrudion, and Llanfairpwllgwyngyll. Can you pronounce them?

- One of the world's biggest food fights is the annual Tomato Battle in the town of Bunol, Spain. The townspeople abandon their table manners and have a wild time throwing 242,000 pounds (110,000 kilograms) of ripe tomatoes at one another.

- France is visited by more tourists each year than any other country in the world.

- London, England, is visited by more tourists each year than any other city in the world.

- Monaco is the most crowded country in the world. It has 37,190 people per square mile (14,349 per square kilometer).

- The Republic of Ireland has half as many people today as it did 150 years ago.

- One of the biggest wetlands in the world is located on the Pripyat River in Belarus. It is as big as the states of New Hampshire and Vermont combined.

- More than thirty thousand stone columns stand packed together like fat, unsharpened pencils at the Giant's Causeway on the northwest coast of northern Ireland.

- The tiny mountain country of Liechtenstein lies along the Rhine River between Austria and Switzerland. It is a major producer of false teeth.

- In 1989, the people of Estonia joined hands to form a 400-mile (644-kilometer) human chain across their country to protest being ruled by the Soviet Union.

- Transylvania is a part of Romania that occupies a high plateau between two mountain ranges. The fictional character Dracula was based on Vlad the Impaler, an evil prince who lived near Transylvania in the 15th century and murdered tens of thousands of his subjects.

- Antarctica is one and a half times larger than the United States.

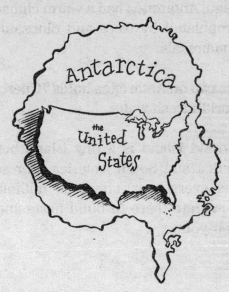

- The ice on Antarctica is more than 1 mile (1.6 kilometers) thick in most places.

- Lake Vostok is a huge lake the size of Lake Ontario that exists 2.5 miles (4 kilometers) under the ice in Antarctica.

- Not all deserts are hot places. Central Antarctica is so dry it is called a polar desert. Only about 2 inches (5 centimeters) of snow falls there each year.

- Long ago, Antarctica had a warm climate and was populated by trees and dinosaurs and small mammals.

- The ice cap on Antarctica holds 70 percent of the world's fresh water.

- Zavadovski Island is a tiny island between Antarctica and South America. For several months every year, about 28 million penguins migrate there to build nests and care for their young.

- The world's windiest place is Common-wealth Bay in Antarctica. Wind speeds there reach 200 miles (320 kilometers) per hour.

- Not all of Antarctica is iced over. The continent has three huge basins called the Dry Valleys, where the rocky ground is dotted by the odd patch of snow.

- The South Pole is much colder than the North Pole. The lowest recorded temperature at the South Pole was 50 degrees Fahrenheit (28 degrees Celsius) colder than the lowest recorded temperature at the North Pole.

- Antarctica has no cities or permanent residents.

- Antarctica has two active volcanoes.

- Half of the people who live in Africa are under 15 years of age.

- The Namib Desert in southern Africa is one of the world's driest and hottest places. Baboons that live there go for weeks without drinking water. To keep cool, the baboons shower themselves with wet sand dug up from underground.

- The "soda lakes" in Kenya and Tanzania are pink, pea-green, and white in color and fizz constantly with air bubbles.

- The Ngorongoro is a dead volcano in Tanzania with an enormous crater that is home to tens of thousands of animals — hippos, warthogs, giraffes, ostriches, rhinos, monkeys, and many others.

- A herd of elephants enters the Kitum Caves in Kenya's Mount Elgon every night. For several hours, the elephants chip away at the caves' walls with their tusks, breaking off chunks of salt, which the elephants eat.

- Towering over the Ahaggar (a region the size of France situated in the middle of the Sahara Desert) are hundreds of bare mountains that look like gigantic, brown bunches of asparagus standing on end.

- "The loneliest country on Earth" is what some people have called the country of Western Sahara. Fewer people live there per square mile than in any other country on Earth.

- The tallest sand dunes in the Sahara are higher than the Empire State Building in New York City.

- Many pygmies live in the magnificent Ituri Forest of Zaire. The ground there is soft and easy to walk on, and the enormous trees are covered with fuzzy vines and "air" plants that rest on the topmost branches like shaggy pussycats.

- All twins born in Nigeria, be they boys or girls, are given the same names. The first-born twin is always named Taiwo, the second born, Kehinde.

- The world's longest river is the Nile in Africa. If you stretched the Nile River across the United States, it would run from Los Angeles almost to New York.

- The world's highest bungee jump platform overlooks Victoria Falls on the border of Zambia and Zimbabwe. The falls are more than 300 feet (91 meters) high and bungee-jumping over them has been called "suicide without dying."

- The Tsingy is a spooky area of needlelike rocks on the African island of Madagascar. The rocks are so sharp there that no one dares walk on them for fear of falling and getting stabbed to death. Some of the rocks are 100 feet (30 meters) tall.

- The world's saltiest body of water is Lake Assal in the country of Djibouti. Its water is clear turquoise and hundreds of natural salt sculptures dot its shoreline.

- The world's tiniest national park, Saiwa Swamp in Kenya, is only 1 mile (1.6 kilometers) square. In this park, a species of antelope called the sitatunga spends its days underwater in the swamp with only its nose poking above the surface.

- The tallest mountain on Earth is Mauna Kea in Hawaii. Measured from its bottom on the sea floor, Mauna Kea is 32,884 feet (10,023 meters) tall.

- Easter Island in the Pacific Ocean got its name because it was discovered by European sailors at Easter time.

- Not all countries are part of a continent. New Zealand, Tonga, Fiji, and several other countries are part of Oceania, a group of about 25,000 islands in the Pacific Ocean.

- Surprise Rock Island in the South China Sea is the newest island in the world. It was first sighted on April 14, 1988.

- "Aa" is what people call the rough, jagged volcanic rock on the Hawaiian islands. The name comes from the cry of pain that barefoot people utter while walking across it.

- The Sargasso Sea is a region in the North Atlantic Ocean that is 2 million square miles (5.2 million square kilometers) in area. Thick mats of seaweed float on the surface there, and small marine animals such as crabs, shrimp, and barnacles live on the seaweed.

- A hill in New Zealand is called Taumatawhakatangihangakoauauotamateaturipukakapikimaungahoronukupokaiwhenuakitanatahu. It means "The place where Tamatea, the man with the big knees, who slid, climbed and swallowed mountains, known as landeater, played his flute to his loved one."

- The "middle of nowhere" is a great expanse of nothing but water in the south Pacific Ocean. It is located 1,600 miles (2,575 kilometers) south of Pitcairn Island, the nearest piece of land.

- More than 850 separate languages are spoken in Papua, New Guinea.

• The horse latitudes are regions in the ocean that are unusually calm. They got their name from old sailing ships carrying horses that got stranded in the calm waters. When freshwater supplies on board ran low, the horses were thrown overboard to save the water for the sailors.

- The deepest known place in the world is the Mariana Trench in the western Pacific Ocean. It is 36,198 feet (11,033 meters) below sea level.

- No one has ever climbed any of the mountains in the world's longest mountain range, the Mid-Atlantic chain. That's because it is underwater in the Atlantic Ocean.

- The bikini bathing suit is named after Bikini Atoll, an island made of coral in the Pacific Ocean.

- A yazoo is a tributary of a river that runs alongside the river.

- There are 28 towns and cities named Springfield in Canada and the United States combined.

- Russia and Turkey are the only countries in the world that lie on two continents. Both countries are part of Europe and Asia.

- The Japanese call their country "Nippon," which means "origin of the sun."

- North America is not directly north of South America. Atlanta, Georgia, is actually farther west than the entire South American continent.

- The Alps in Europe are not the only Alps mountains in the world. There are Alps mountain chains in both Australia and New Zealand.

- The citizens of Centralia, Pennsylvania, won't move out of town, even though the ground deep beneath their homes is burning. A fire in an old coal mine started the ground burning in 1962. The townspeople refuse to budge despite warnings from the government that their lives are in danger.

- In the Northern Hemisphere, tornadoes spin counterclockwise; in the Southern Hemisphere, they spin clockwise.

- Millions of years ago, North America, Europe, and Asia were once part of a huge continent that modern scientists call Laurasia. Africa, South America, Australia, and Antarctica were part of another huge continent called Gondwana.

- The wind blows millions of tons of dust more than 2,000 miles (3,600 kilometers) from the Sahara Desert across the Atlantic Ocean to South America every year. The dust settles on the ground and fertilizes plants that grow in the Amazon River basin.

- Flying nonstop from San Francisco to New York takes longer than flying nonstop from New York to San Francisco. Because the planet rotates from west to east, a plane flies farther when traveling from San Francisco to New York. The increase in distance increases the flying time.

- No one will ever climb Peary's Crocker Land, a mountain range in the Arctic. The mountains are a mirage, caused by the reflection of sunlight on the ice.

- Many sand dunes around the world "sing" — they make loud booming and roaring noises. Scientists haven't figured out what causes the noises.

- Seventy-one percent of all the land on Earth is north of the equator.

- Amerigo Vespucci was an Italian explorer who claimed to have reached what is now the United States before Christopher Columbus did. The word "America" comes from Vespucci's first name.

- Earth is not perfectly round. It is slightly squashed at the North and South poles.

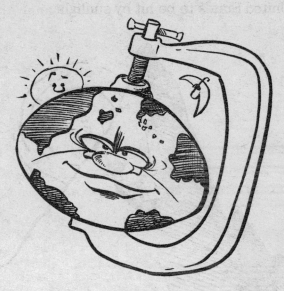

- Nome, Alaska, got its name by mistake. An early mapmaker did not know the name of a certain town in Alaska, so he penciled in "Name?" on his map. Someone misread "Name" as "Nome" and the error stuck.

- Simooms and haboobs are fierce whirlwinds that race through deserts in North Africa and Arabia.

- On a clear morning, the top of Mount Katahdin in Maine is the first place in the United States to be hit by sunlight.

- Pingos are cone-shaped hills in the Arctic. They appear wherever water underground freezes and makes the earth bulge. A large pingo may take centuries to grow.

- The word *geography* comes from the Greek language and means "earth description."

Hugh Westrup writes for *Current Science*, a children's classroom magazine. He has visited six Canadian provinces, twenty-five U.S. states, and nine countries in Europe.